The Horse
And
The Girl

The Horse
And
The Girl

Book I of The Crossing Places Series

poems

Madeleine F White

Sea Crow Press

BY MADELEINE F WHITE

Mother Of Floods

To my beautiful Lucie Horse,
who helped me find my way back to myself.

CONTENTS

The Horse
And
The Girl

THE GIRL ON THE HORSE

"I can't breathe" said
the Girl who sat on
the Horse who strode on
the Road that distributed load
and covered The Earth.
I grieve

"No more can I carry" said
the Horse with
the Girl who sat on his back on
the Road that distributed load
and covered The Earth.
Too long have we tarried

"I am dead" said
the Road that covered
the Earth which had given birth to
the Girl and the Horse.
"I was never alive you know."
I'm not part of your daily bread

"I'm alive" said
the Earth murmuring under the road
"I distribute the load and hold what is green and unseen
in the dark of my womb to bring forth life."
Together we thrive

"But if you keep covering all I am and will be –
my forest, my fields and my seas
with things that are dead,
the Girl on the Horse will not catch a breath,
and we'll all be dead, as a matter of course".
You see?

FUN

"Giddy up!" said the Girl
"Let's have a run
I'm looking for joy today!"

She dropped in her stirrups
and kicked on the Horse
who agreed it was time to play.

AGE

I'm no longer young, said the Girl to the Horse
unless I'm in the field with you
I get hot flushes and don't remember
all the things I need to do.

"Well, think of this,"
said the Horse to the Girl
"The same applies to me,
at 18 or so," he gave a harrumph,
"Things aren't quite as they used to be."

"You give me glucosamine for my joints and
balancer to keep me going
then turmeric as a general thing
and garlic to keep my blood flowing."

He gave her a slanted sideways glance
then came the killer line
"What do you do to look after yourself?"
Said the Girl, "I don't have the time."

"There's my point," said the Horse,
"You bemoan your age
but do little to make you feel better –
you depend on me and HRT
and your dear old cable knit sweater."

"Go have a dance, meet with some friends
rewrite your night with a better end
no aching joints or empty nest
instead, just do what you love best..."

He threw back his head rearing up for the filly
who'd come to the fence to watch him being silly
"Take the Girl by the hand, lead her through the gate
you might feel a bit older but it's never too late!"

PEOPLE

"It's odd, you know",
said the Horse to the Girl
"You people are such a puzzle."

"Tell me more said the girl,"
while combing his mane
and stroking his velvety muzzle.

"Well," Said the Horse,
"It's your world of course
or at least that's what you think
but all that busyness, rushing around
is driving us to the brink."

"What do you mean?"
said the Girl to the Horse
sporting a puzzled frown
I do my work and I come here to play
and in between fill a challenging day
by trying to fix my surrounds.

"But what if you're fixing the things that don't matter
and breaking the things that do?
Who cares whether so and so hates getting fatter
and the other one doesn't like you?"

"Look at me said the horse"
proudly sporting a crest
that had hardened with fat through the grass
"I don't care if I'm fat, I don't like being thin
but I'm part of a world made to last."

"Are you saying I'm spinning too fast?"
asked the girl. At that, he glared very hard,
"Your feet never touch the ground without me
you're always looking but you cannot see –
the deep blue skies, the sparrowhawk's flight
the red of the sunset stretching into the night...

"Stop!" shouted the girl, I hear what you're saying
those things are nice
but they're part of playing."
And she brushed away curls with her sweaty palms
realising she was no longer calm –

"Real life is all about building and doing
where do you think I get the money for shoeing?
To pay for you and this lovely green field
I need to rush all the time
to fit in, to yield..."

"Stop!" whinnied the horse
"It's time to trust
that if you let it all go
you'll be good enough.
The earth will still spin,
the spiders still weave
the tides come and go
you just need to believe –
that the slow song of power

you hear from my back
is always there, always ready
just develop the knack...

of making deep truths from the earth come to you
by serving the good – and the beautiful, too!"

He gave her a shove which made her think
'The Horse can lead me to water
but it's my choice to drink.'

CAN'T SEE FOR LOOKING

"I can't see said the Girl
there's too much to do,"
as she rode on the Horse one day.

She bent down to pat
the broad dappled back
and put her phone away.

Said the Horse loud and clear,
"Look through my ears
that will restrict your view –
you'll still see what matters,
the Sky and Path
as they stretch out in front of you."

He twisted his neck to reach the green grass
and crunched on the bit in content
then swivelled his eyes to make quite sure
that she understood what he meant.

"But don't look behind,
or fear the bends out in front
as you might forget where we're going."
"Ah I see," said the Girl
as she patted the Horse –

"Sometimes it's better not knowing."

THE PATH

When they'd ridden a while
she pulled up with a smile
and said "I'm a Girl you're a Horse
he twitched back an ear
his puzzlement clear
"I've known that for some time, of course."

Indeed, said the girl,
and just so we're clear
though, I think it's fantastic my horse is sarcastic
will you lend me a listening ear?

The Horse settled down with a snort and a frown
and the Girl proceeded to say
"I wanted to know, as a Horse and a Girl,
whether we see things the same way?"

"For example, the path we're coming to now…"
"This one, you mean, beside scary cows?"
"That's exactly my point," the Girl answered briskly
"To you they loom large, to me their quite spiffy."

"Well for me", said the Horse
"One foot follows the other
if the road is hard my hooves make a clatter
if the path is soft, either mud or grass
it means we can go extremely fast."

"But I don't like things like the scary cows
or the cat that jumps out with a sudden miaow
or the rubbish that's tipped from the side of the road
a car surreptitiously dumping its load."

"Yes", said the Girl, "I remember that well!
You took the reins and we galloped a spell
I was very scared…""Well so was I!" said the horse
I don't like things from an undefined source.

"So what about when we go somewhere new
and there's lots of stuff that might scare you?"
Said the girl with a short tap of both of her heals
and he moved off so fast, that she let out a squeal –

"Well then," he said with a snort and a huff
"I depend on the fact you know your stuff
I trust you, and though, I'm still very wary
of the things by the path that can be quite scary
if you're OK, I am generally too
because when we're together I know what to do."

He stopped at a puddle and started drinking
and she said, "I like your way of thinking.
You mean we're at one when I'm on your back,
with the courage to face the more challenging hacks?"

The wind caught his words as he huffed his reply
and the power of its breath brought a tear to her eye.
"Not just the hack but our path every day
together we're safe, no matter what comes our way."

THE SOUND OF SILENCE

"Be still," says the Girl, "I want to listen
to the wind that makes
the ice-christened branches
clatter in the hard frost,
Squirrel chasing along them after the nut he lost."

So they ride on.
hushed stillness following them –
swallowing them.

And the twig cracks
and the saddle creaks
and the kestrel cries
and the Earth sighs.

Heavily, moistly the laden Sky hangs
over a hard earthen crust. Violence masked.
Eat or be eaten, roots twisting
mice nesting, moles digging
genesis of life in the sound of silence.

And the branch breaks
and the saddle creaks
and the kestrel cries
and the Horse breathes.

Listen to the darkness.
Clanging against the hazy grey
of the Road
heavy tyres masking the vastness
of what lies beneath.

And the stream seeps
and the saddle creaks
and the rook rattles
and the jackdaw cackles.

Life is formed in darkness
and like the shiny toys of a magpie
light can be just noise
sometimes shining so brightly
it hides the truth.

A distant dog barks, an icicle cracks.
Horse's hooves clatter
as it shatters.

THE GIFT HORSE

"I remember the red scarf tied round my head
and the words of the farmer's daughter
'Sei still. Be still.' And I was, the Girl said.

"In her strong arms on that broad-backed mare
I felt safe and free – even at three,
I knew what mattered, you see."

Said the Horse,
"I remember my first field.
The mare shadowing wobbly steps
and the Boy watching in wonder
as our worlds enmeshed."

The Girl closed her eyes.
"I remember the forest loam,
the sandstone rocks, pink and red,
the German home I adored.
And Fauni, the sturdy Icelandic pony
helping me to explore."

"I remember the harness, the pulling"
Horse's brown eyes shot through with pain
"My smart trot, the Boy
older now – nearly man
driving me along lanes
then the smashing and crashing.
Eye bleeding, leg hurting."

"I remember the hurting."
Still-burnished memories speak through green eyes.
"When I came to English shores
though I spoke the language
words baffled and confounded
I was no longer grounded.
'Here' didn't feel like home anymore."

Said the Horse, "I remember different places.
Fast people, fast lorries, the aloneness –
despite all the faces.
Though I still spoke the same language
nobody heard like before
I wasn't anyone's Boy anymore."

"I remember," said the Girl.
"When even wings imaginary
no longer carried me.
More-fool rides as little asides."

Horse shifted his weight.
"I remember the waiting.
Though I had grass and water most of the time
for years, nobody was there to call mine
I was fleet of foot and hard of mouth.
Feared."

Then you came.

Said Girl,
"I was the same.
I was frightened and quietened
travelling constantly,
no time to be
I'd become ill,
still."

Then you came.

"A January day, just like today
bleak and grey
but there you stood.
Unshod, held in the sod."

"A January day, just like today
you brushed and fussed
though you couldn't hear me yet,
I felt the catalogue of years through
the wetness of your tears."

"Then," breathed the Girl
"As I let go of the life I'd once known
I started hearing you –
exchanging minds-eye memories of dark-forest loam
for the Kent Coast's spirit song,
made home."

They were still for a while
he leant on her, she on him
thoughts journeying on
as the winter sky dimmed.

Then he turned with a nudge
his breath warm on her face
"and it certainly helps that you know your place..."

Tone now brimming with cheeky delight,
he decided to add one final aside.
"If I'm as precious as you say
then what about a treat today?"

And his Gift horse's mouth opened wide.

WILL YOU WALK INTO THIS HORSEBOX?

"Will you walk into this horsebox?"
Said the Girl so sweetly-voiced,
"Climbing up into my lorry
is, of course, your direct choice.
But flaps are down, the walkway bare
your feed-bowl's in – look its right there…"

"Oh no, no, no, puffed big bold horse
"To ask me is in vain
for who goes in that lorry
will ne'er come down again."

"I'm sure you must be tired dear,
with all the work you've done."
She waved a juicy carrot, as though marshalling his run,
"If you come up and look inside, we'll soon be on our way
it's cool and dark, just rest a while on this nice bed of hay."

"Oh no, no, no, snorted big bold horse
for I've often heard it said
that going in a lorry
messes with your head."

Said the cunning Girl unto the Horse
"Dear friend, what can I do –
to show the things awaiting us?
Look, here's a timely clue."
She pulled out a blue rosette and waved it with a flourish,
"Come, glory is awaiting,
you just need a little courage!"

"Oh no, no, no pawed big bold horse
dear Girl, that's not for me
competitions are so boring
here is better, don't you see?

"My darling Horse", said Girl quite loud
and now through gritted teeth
while he stared at her blankly: no quarter, no reprieve.
"We'll see new things and have some fun
meet with more friends, go on a run….
Please listen when I say that
coming in this lorry will brighten up your day!"

"I thank you so", said Horse to Girl
"You are extremely kind… I'd rather not –
if it's OK, I'll just stay behind."

FEET OF CLAY

The Girl's feet were like clay
as she walked up the field
losing her boots in the mud
she didn't notice her Horse
the lithe figure he cut
instead, she looked down at the sod.

"Why aren't you speaking?"
said the Horse to the Girl
"I'm missing our cheerful banter.
The sky is blue and the ground is soft
I want to go out for a canter."

"I'm sad and I'm tired doing what is required
lost in the 'shoulds' and the 'musts'
it's wet and its cold and I'm getting old
and I'm sick of not making the cut.

A harrumphing snort, was his retort
brown eyes meeting green.
"Then come for a run and we'll have some fun
and you can work out how to be seen."

Said the Girl to the Horse,
"I don't know if I can, not even you are listening!"
Said the Horse to the Girl
"Find that other place,
where you can feel the raindrops' glistening."

"There the ground is soft, and I've plenty of hay
and the birds in the sky have lots to say.

Said the Girl, "So I just need to try?"

THE HORSE AND THE DOG

Said the Horse to the Dog
"You inveterate snob
why are you barking at me?"

"Your Man is silly, all booted and suited
and the hat is pure frippery."

"My Girl's hat is hard, and she sits up straight
while her body bends like a tree
and we fly under trees and over the stream
and not even you can catch me!"

The Dog barked once, in loud disgust
and turned with a snarl and a growl
"You big oafen beast
on you I will feast
and under the moon I will howl!"

With a flick of his tail and a stamp of his foot
the Horse signalled utter disdain
"My hooves are hard
and my eyes are sharp
don't let me see you again!"

Said the Girl to her Horse
when she noticed he'd shied
at the sound of the Man's clicking tongue
"Never mind them my dear,
leave them shackled by mud,
and the silliness they have begun."

And they spun as they stood,
running into the wood
wind whistling through trees by the water.

Said the Horse to the Girl
"That showed them – you'll see!"
And she rocked in the saddle with laughter.

RAGWORT

"What are you doing?" said the Horse to the Girl
"I'm clearing the field," said she

"It's early summer and the Ragwort is sprouting
as far as the eye can see."

"Don't worry said Horse; I'm not stupid you know
I know what I can and can't eat –"

"This meadow is deliciously full
and that's not my idea of a treat!"

The girl looked up, mopping her brow
it was hot work on her knees with a fork and trowel

"You can see it's growing between the grass
and If I don't catch it, it'll keep spreading fast"

"I won't eat it, I tell you, I never have done
I need my liver and pain isn't fun!"

A little hop sideways signalled contempt
then he nibbled around it to show what he meant.

The Girl now turned fully, squinting through the sun's
brightness, "I'll clear all I see, despite your lack of politeness."

She pointed at her barrow and the ragwort heaped there
it's leaves shrivelling up in the sun's hot glare

"That was me up in town, I felt tired and mangled

down on my knees, pulling roots that were tangled."

"There, the ragwort was digital,
much worse than physical..."

"So, even though, you're not keen on my digging
and these roots knot through soil like uncontrolled rigging..."

"At least here I can see the space that I've cleared
watch the plants that I've pulled heaping up unimpaired"

"But as far as thankless tasks go – and in life there are many"
(arching eyebrows at him because Horse offered plenty!)

"It's a pain picking a field clean of this stuff
and for today, I say, enough is enough!"

He turned his head, lazily catching her eye
watching her throw the fork down with a sigh.

"But at least here, there's physical proof of success
and it makes my life feel like less of a mess."

With total disinterest the Horse showed her his bottom
what did it matter that before him, she'd felt rotten?

DUCHESS

"My name is Duchess, but call me Dee
and that's the girl looking after me."
The bay mare nodded across their heads
to a scrawny young woman by the lean-to shed.

"I once was Duchess, the Diamond Horse
that was my name on the track, of course,
in my halcyon days I was the darling of racing
but these days, I really am quite self-effacing."

She paused for breath, but then ploughed on
Horse looked at the girl – it was time to be gone!
Muttering under his breath as he jerked to escape
"That mare is not a racing shape
more a Clydesdale cross, if you ask me"
and he pulled again, most determinedly.

"Oh yes, I was famous county-wide
and wore my master's colours with pride
but now I'm feeling completely undone –
all alone and woebegone!"

Said the Girl with a sharp glance as Horse rolled his eyes.
"Well, at least you're here now, and she seems very nice."

"Well, that's where you're wrong!"
Said Dee with a snort
"She's the love 'em and leave 'em sort.
Since we got here, I've been all on my own
stuck by this lorry and so far from home.
She hasn't even been over to see
if this is a place that works for me."

Dee sighed again and Horse made his escape
Girl's tap on his sides not a moment too late.
But, to his horror, when they reached the field
he saw the woman had come to his gate!

"I'd best be sociable don't you think?
And say hello, while I'm here."
Said the Girl, while quickly untacking him
said the Horse," Don't tell her I'm here!"

"I think she knows," chuckled Girl to the Horse
while patting his mud-streaked rump
"I'll find out why Dee's still tied up over there –
no wonder she's got the hump."

The woman's poor attempt at a smile
told Girl that that something was wrong
"We've been for travelling hours and my Sat Nav broke
I'm out by miles – it's such a joke!
but the new owner won't be too long."

Girl stayed to watch her bring Dee across
while juggling lead rope and phone.
Said the woman,
"He's texted he's coming soon
but I'd best be getting along."

Girl stayed till the evening waiting with Dee
and noticed how lame she was
until in the end it became apparent
that no one was coming because –
she was just another old horse.

THE NATURE OF THINGS

Hazy heat hung over the Road
as Girl drove through the shimmering grey
it seemed as though Road was sweating too –
it felt like a very odd day.

She got to the field and saw standing there
shiny-smart by the heavy main gate
a great sign announcing, 'Land Acquired, Enquiries'
and then a date...

Girl parked the car and walked down the track
through fields that seemed oddly quiet,
'My mind is racing but I've lost the knack
of doing what is required'.

Duchess was standing next to her gate
the Farmer had let her stay
"After all," he said with very good grace
"Field's empty and the last ones left hay."

Girl patted her nose, but got no reply
what was going on?
And then despite a very lame leg
Dee trotted off, keen to be gone.

'No sign of Horse' thought Girl pushing through
some wires come loose in his fence
but then she reasoned, he'll be sheltering from
this heat, if he's got any sense!

She found where he was and, as a sensible horse,
he had indeed found a place inside
but when she got closer, she found to her horror,
he was sporting a bloody great bite!

"Horse, what happened? Tell me right now!"
Her words came in a bit of a shout,
"This bite on your neck did not just appear
and how on earth did you get out!?"

"That damned mare came on heat
and she had the gall
to bite me for following nature's call!"

"Flipping heck!" said the Girl,
so you mounted Dee,
she's so much bigger that you –
you're lucky there wasn't any more damage
she's 17 hands to your 14'2!

Horse sulked and was silent
while Girl cleaned and sprayed
other than exclaiming "It stings!"
This gave the Girl the chance to turn
her mind to the nature of things.

And the way the Road keeps unfolding itself
over life's green earthen core
human nature at the heart of it all –
with its constant desire for more.

WHAT ABOUT DEATH?

The Girl watched a bee
fallen into the tub
that was filled with water to drink.
"What about death?"
she said to the Horse
and he said,
"I need to think."

So, she settled on lawn, cropped short by his teeth
and warmed by the balmy sun
closing her eyes, from the silenced surmised
the answer'd take a while to come.

The dream-galloped hooves and his flying mane
made the Girl raise a close-lidded smile
but after a while she felt a warm breath
coming at her from over the stile.

"I have thought," said the Horse
"But while we're alive
why are you thinking of death?"

"Remember the fox we passed every day
and the air that was once his breath?
Now stinking and rotting into the road
his flesh all that's left of his mortal load."

The Girl nodded once
she remembered him well
the greying fur and the terrible smell.
Pleased she was listening with all of her ears
the Horse continued
stepping up to be near.

"In the shadow of death
it's our soul that rots
our hardships magnified
because all the time we are living in fear
the life-giving spark in us dies."

"But if like that bee we struggle and fight
demanding the most from each day
then the moment of death can hold us no more
and we soon soar up and away."

Said the girl as she looked in the dusty trough,
"You are wise my beautiful boy
a silver train carried me time and again
to a life devoid of joy."

"But I'm no longer there,
instead, I'm here –
feet planted firm on the Earth
though I've felt the power of a living death
you've shown me what my life is worth."

SEASCAPE

The crane on the coast shards the sky.
A scythe, cutting the horizon
connecting fields and sea.

The widowed mast mirroring
the smaller one behind Horse's shelter –
still standing fast against the welter of activity
and the builders' proclivity
to churn up all they see.

"Let's ride to the beach" Girl suggests,
"Less noise, less mess."

Horse agrees and they set off.
Past blue boarding and hoardings
picking their way between
builders and diggers
the mounds of soil getting bigger and bigger
holding the Earth at bay.

Keeping the crane on the shore in their sights
they trot towards it as the fracturing light
sparkles invitingly.

The path to the sea leads through woodlands and marshes
Road halted in its tracks.
'But for how long?' wonders Girl as they ride,
muttering, "It's not worth looking back."

Marsh harriers soar and serene swans glide
delightful distractions on this coastal ride.

"Nearly there" says the Girl as the path starts to unravel
pebbles shooting away from their direction of travel.
"Remember the salt from the sea is good
for hardening hooves, especially now you're unshod."

But the wind blows harder the closer they get
and the Horse starts blowing too,
the shifting surroundings making him fret
and the Girl is unsure what to do.
Still, she kicks on towards the waves
telling Horse sternly, "It's time to behave."

Horse, though, isn't keen on waves crashing
and doesn't fancy the water bashing his legs.
He likes it being still and smooth; whispering, glistening,
instead.

Girl says crossly, "This nonsense must stop!"
and brushes his rump with a rarely used crop
Horse takes affront and off he goes
into the water with a torpedoing nose
his nostrils flaring, he puts his ears back,
and Girls' composure begins to crack.

"Stop!" she shouts wildly, "You're no submarine"
"I take it all back" and "What a good Boy you've been!"
But Horse is insensible to Girl's voice in the din
the waves get higher and then, she falls in.

At last, he halts and turns around
snorting and puffing – distress still profound.
Girl gets to her feet, sea up to her chest
"OK, I concede that you know best..."

As they make their way back, she adds
voice no longer subdued: "That is, unless I do..."

FACES

"Personhood is misunderstood"
says the Girl – as she starts tracing
a finger along the soft cheek she is facing.

Making much of her touch the Horse replies,
"With people the familiar is closely guarded
and what's not similar, quickly discarded.

"But if you change the definition
to one of recognition –
a mirror image creates where hate fades."

HELL FOR LEATHER

The rumbling lorry rolled along the road
as the Girl and the Horse trotted on
"Will he slow, I wonder, and let us past?"
Muttered Girl to the Horse, as the horn gave a blast.

The wheels thundered closely, the contents were rattling
Horse took the reins and the Girl started battling.
He'd relented a little, and she felt a bit stronger
when the blast came again, and this one was longer!

Quick as a flash Horse put down his head
Girl's hands were like steel but her stomach was lead.
She knew what was coming, she'd been there before
but not on a road, with its hard, tarmacked core.

'Must pull', thought the Girl, to the fields at the side
'move across, move across, for a safer ride.'

"Help!" squealed Horse, "Must run very fast
away from the traffic that's flying past."

"The lorry, the cars, the noise and the clatter..."
'Help, help!' thought the Girl 'If I fall, I will shatter!'

Steel-shod hooves crashed; sparks continued to fly
fear's void caught Girl's scream of, "We're going to die."

A pull to the left, the will to stay in one piece
one sharp, strong tug – then the release.

Shooting onto the pavement and into the maize
the Horse and the Girl continued their race.

The tall stems broke as the pair crashed through
paces eating the ground as Horse panicked anew
but once again she pulled to the left
'If he sprints round in circles, he'll soon run out of breath.'

And sure enough, as the circles tightened
his pace started slowing and he seemed less frightened
her knuckles still white, Girl released a little
no longer feeling so desperately brittle.

'If I fall now,' she took a deep breath,
I'll crash and I'll hurt, but it doesn't mean death.
As her body softened Horse took his cue,
his fright and flight impulse dying down too.

Flanks heaving and foaming (and that was just her!)
Horse stood four-square with sweat-sodden fur.
Girl slid from the saddle, all boneless and formless
patting half-tonne Horse, who now stood there.
Quite harmless.

Girl shook and she sobbed and her heart beat faster
she'd not held Horse but had averted disaster.

A Man and a Dog came up to her side
they'd tried to follow the madcap ride
from roadside to field, "Our own safety not heeded"
him and Dog had come, "Just in case we were needed."

Dog didn't bark, his eyes watchful and still
as the Man pointed up through the rain to the hill.
"You did a good job, holding Horse today
just across there is the motorway."

"But the next time you want to go hell for leather
maybe check for soft ground and better weather."
He doffed his hat as he patted her arm,
"But me and Dog here, we're pleased you weren't harmed."

HORSE SENSE

She shovelled a handful of Kalms with one hand
the other one clutching the wheel
manoeuvring her little Toyota through traffic
in a bid to get to the field.

It had been a few weeks since the lorry had caused
that close call with the road and the traffic
"I just need to remember how I feel when I'm on him,
that riding makes me ecstatic."

But these days their conversation was lacking
her heart racing when she came near him,
the good memories marred by the lack of control
and the length of his stride and her terrified soul…

The sense of being at one with the Horse
her 'power and glory self', gone
replaced by a shadow of how she once was
she was determined to get back on!

She mixed calming cookies into his feed
and ate a couple herself
'After all,' she thought, 'they're OK for him
so they're bound to be good for my health.'

Then picking his hooves she brushed his coat
untangling burrs from his mane
and lifting the saddle onto his back
she added the bit and the reins.

Her heart in her mouth, her foot in the stirrup
blood pulsing through her, as though set for a gallop –
she tried to breathe calmly, not showing fear
despite not knowing if her horse sense was there.

"I'm not going to run, I'm right here with you."
His voice was back, and she knew what to do.
"I'm your Girl, your my Horse
I've been trying to be brave
but now I hear you again I know you'll behave."

He lowered his head, with a soft little snort
her submission acknowledged with one final retort:

"Your heart sounding loud, the thrum of it beating
tells me fear is just fear and its causes are fleeting.
You are mine; I am yours our covenant made
here on earth for now, till our time is repaid."

He turned round to face her; his eyes heaven-deep
determined to make her spirit-self leap:
"Today we will ride with no care for tomorrow
the moment will take us beyond any sorrow
running straight across the fields to the sea
our horizons stretching out infinitely."

PUDDLE DRINKING

The sun beat down from a pitiless blue
the sky glaring and harsh
as heat hit her anew.
It had seemed a great thought
to see the marshes at dawn
but then they'd got lost
and the path carried on…

The ditches and bridges were OK for the hikers
but for a Girl on a Horse not as easy to bypass.
So they'd kept close to the stream
the distant church in their sights,
guided by its tall steeple in the morning light.
Then the horse dipped his head.

There, in front, was a puddle.
He slurped at it so greedily
he got mud on his muzzle.

"What d'you think?" said the Girl,
"Is that something for me?
My throat is so dry it feels papery.
Under this hat it's sweaty and hot
I think I'll try just a little, so don't drink the lot!"

She dismounted, followed by a pair of brown eyes
"You're a Girl, not a Horse I'm not sure that's wise."

"Well," she said, her feet on the ground
"I know we've discussed that, but haven't we found –
that a lot of the things that are good for you
with a bit of adapting work for me too?"
She put in both hands, scooping greedily,
muttering under her breath, "It looks fine to me."

———

Forty-eight hours and the Girl hadn't been
to feed him or brush him or keep his field clean
eventually, turning up a day late,
she said, "My stomach's been dicky,
something I ate..."

Said the Horse to the Girl
"It wasn't food caused the trouble
it was copying me,
drinking from that big puddle."

"Well, whatever the case"
said the Girl with a smile,
"I'll be careful of what I ingest for a while.
This week, I know, has been pretty chaotic
but things are OK now – I've got antibiotics!"

I MADE A MISTAKE

I made a mistake said the Girl to the Horse
"Not the puddle again?" quipped he.
He couldn't resist the cheeky aside
even though he'd promised to let that one slide
the memory still filled him with glee.

"No said the Girl. This one's much worse
I feel pain, right here inside…"
said Horse "Quit the dramatics,
failure's not automatic –
it's more likely your damaged pride."

"I didn't check a key fact and its out on the web
what's worse, it's been discovered!"

"Who by?" said the Horse, as he munched on the grass,
"By the author and he's really bothered…"

"Maybe then, write something else instead?
Our conversations, for instance, get them out of your head."

Having said what he thought, the Horse went back to eating
feeling bad about things was like taking a beating.
But then along came one final idea,
he thought was important for her to hear:
"If you've made a mistake, upon reflection
remember life's about progress, not perfection."

THE MAN AND THE GIRL

The loose-limbed dawn stretched.
Fingers of an early autumn
Grasping their way into the new September day.

Browned detritus crackled on the ground
the long, hot summer meant trees had already shed
part of their leafy crowns.

A cunning spider who'd dared
stretch its web between water-buckets and hedge
had snared an earthworm.

Over the last few days Girl had been amazed
to see how the worm had shrunken and sunken
into a dry pencilled husk and then dust.

The image still running through her mind
Girl worried about the sign
and the people she'd seen coming:
Hard hats, orange vests, papers in hand
plans like spiders' webs stretching across the land.

Her mind still unclear as to where to go,
Girl trusted Horse to follow his nose
so they passed through the village
the new toytown houses on its fringes
uneasy spouses. And the Road stretched.

Horse continued down a tarmacked track
visible only from Horse's back
but otherwise concealed by the
long-stemmed crops spilling from the fields.

A sharp bark took her mind off the sign
and she met the Man's friendly greeting
with her own nodded incline.

"You seem very distracted," he said.
Dog barked his assent; he knew what Man meant.
"Well, the field's been sold off and the farmer's not said
where all the horses will be going instead!"

She hoped the Man might have more information
along with the inclination to share what he knew.

"It's a shame, that's for sure,
and they'll always want more
look how these fields have gone!"
He looked back to the houses
past the path they had ridden
saying sadly, "It'll all be built on."

Said the girl, "I know, but where will we go?
here won't be anywhere left!"
"If it helps" said the Man, "
"I think there's land, but only if you're swift,
down Minster way where the nuns still hold sway.
If you ask them, you might have a chance."

Dog backed away from Horse's legs
obeying admonishing hands
"It's such a shame," the man repeated
"They're making these 'New Town' plans."

"These field's you're on, since the farmer changed
from crops to horses and cattle
there's been new life and I've really enjoyed
watching nature winning her battle."

Asked the Girl, "How d'you mean?"
Replied Man, "Have you seen the
sparrowhawks flying above?
They feed on the moles and the mice and the voles
the field's a true treasure trove!
Then smaller creatures die for them
and the cycle starts all over again..."

"It's been a such a joy to see pesticides yielding and the Earth's
reseeding!"

They were still for a while
'till Girl said with a smile,
"It's good to know things can recover –
maybe in the fulness of time
we'll be more inclined to make space for one another."

Dog barked again, and as they moved on
Horses' pace changed from a walk to a run.
But Girl still managed to hear Man's voice say,
"Be prepared, Dog tells me, a hard frost's on its way."

YOU MAGNIFICENT BEAST

"Will you still love me?"
asked the Horse of the Girl
"When I can't run anymore
no longer galloping on the wind
with my hooves thundering loud on the shore?"

"You magnificent beast"
said the Girl to the Horse
"I love you with all of my heart
I can't imagine that day
but just let me say
that's when I do my part."

"Through all these years you have carried me,
brave and bold and true
and when I couldn't carry myself
I depended on you."

"Together we'll hang up our riding boots
and enjoy the glorious green
the Earth will be there
and the sun will still shine
and together we'll gallop through infinite time
into the world of dreams.

THE GREEN MAN

"I've heard it say that fairies play with every raindrop that falls
and that there's a Green Man in the wood
who comes when nature calls."

"I've heard it say," said Girl to Horse
continuing with her tale,
"That every time a tree is felled
a banshee starts to wail."
Said Horse, "I think you're mixing lore –
not to mention metaphors!"

"But still, with the rain sheeting through backlit clouds
while we're here beneath the trees
it's fun to look and name and share
the things we might like to see."

"I've heard it say," said Horse to Girl
"A waft of the woodland loam
is not just an olfactory call
but the Earth's voice summoning us home".

"I've heard it say," the Girl went on
running with theme and idea
"That when a fox runs across your path
the time for change is near."

"I've heard it say," said Horse shaking his head
loos'ning glistening drops from his mane,
"That the forest holds the secret of life,
the depth of its green sharing how to survive
because nothing stays the same."

"That's good to know," said Girl to Horse
"And if you were less of a pain
we could go in a lorry and explore true forest
instead of this small woodland lane."

They were both silent.
The wet prickled and trickled
off noses and branches
and, following myriad dances,
rain's rivulets entered the Earth.

"I'd like to say," said Horse after a while
that though I'm full of fear,
I know I'll have to go in some time
as the change that is coming is near."
With that he attempted a horsey grin –
"Maybe the Green Man himself will lead me in!"

THE HOLE IN THE FENCE

The frost had hit hard
spiky grass poking white
'till Girl's boots crushed the delicate filigree.

The ground was hard
though not quite frozen
it's silver-crusted mantle stretching as far as the eye could see.

Horse's breath greeted her, clouds of it
meeting her on the way to his shelter.

It was too early for workmen
so, with the rickety planking enveloping them
the pair were able to see crackling silence plume across the
fields.

They prepared for the ride inside.
"The Dog foretold the cold," said the Horse.

"Though I did think there'd be longer to wait"
said the Girl, on their way to the gate.

Frost-rimed, Dee stood close by
Horse snorted and she retorted
with a whinnying sigh:

"When I stopped riding out it wasn't by choice."
Girl noticed the catch in Dee's voice,
"They said it was better,
but for whom? It came to soon…"

Just then, through a hole in the fence:
Triangle face, copper coat,
masked vulpine stare aimed at the mare
wide-plumed tail that seemed to float
as air-soft paws padded across.

Fox eyes flickering green
held the promise of places unseen
so, Duchess followed him out.

MOON SONG

Horse and Girl and Dee one night stared up at the silvery Moon
the crystal light spilling over them accompanying his age-old
tune.

"Where are you going and what do you wish?"
He demanded of the three –

"We want to see the spoon and the dish
and the cow jumping beautifully
but if not," shouted Girl,
aiming up at the stars
"Make sure your blessing isn't too far
from where we're called to be."

"And even when going into the dark,"
said Dee, her eyes filled with strange light,
"Give us the strength to see it through
with steadfastness, force and might."

"And Moon," said the Horse, "Just one last thing
while you're singing this lullaby
keep shining your light upon these fields
as the rest of the world passes by."

DEFINITES

"I don't like not knowing where I'm going," said Horse.
Replied Girl, "I'm like that too –
however, the time is very close
when that's exactly what we'll need to do.

Horse laid back his ears, and rolled his eyes
"I like definite absolutes –
the same sun rising above the field
makes me feel more resolute."

"I do understand," and Girl reached her hand
to scratch Horse behind his left ear,
"But in my years I have found
the more you cling to surrounds
the more you have to fear."

Said Horse, "But you wearing your orange vest
as a signal we're heading out
and the little black pouch with its lovely treats
that's what my life's about!"

Girl traced soft fingers down the blaze
shining white from his beautiful face.
"That won't change" she said,
her voice sweet and low –
"You must know, that wherever we go,
this will always be your place."

One hand on her heart, the other his chest
she added a further thought,
"Gratitude for all we've been and seen,
is what our time here has taught."

"And as for our adventures and chats –
I hope you've written them down
You must remember, you promised me that!"
Added the Horse with a frown.

He turned his head to glance at Dee,
back from her adventures, grazing peacefully.
"Where is she going? Is she staying with me?"
His question trailed wistfully.

Girl replied, "I think you know so,
let's make the most of her
before we go."

THE BIRDS

They rode out one day and saw a Swan
he hissed at them: "Where have the marshes gone?"

They rode out one day and saw a Rook
he cawed: "Look at all the land they took!"

They rode out one day to the scream of a Hawk:
"They said they would save us, but it was just talk."

They rode out one day and saw a Crow
he said: "Get yourselves ready it's time to go..."

THE DISAPPEARED FIELD

Man patted Dog as the boards went up
hiding the last of the fields
"Well, that's that, the horses are gone
a new era's being revealed."

"I hope the gelding found a place with the nuns
and that the big mare enjoyed one last day in the sun…"

"It's such a shame. I hear she was quiet though, when they
came."

"Ordinary houses for ordinary people
not much room left for us, eh?"
He turned away.

THE SHADOW HORSE

"Mummy Mummy, the horse is here
look out there by the tree!"
"I can't see anything," said his mum,
"It looks like shadows to me."

"But Mummy he's there
and he wants me to come
down to the field to play and run."

"My darling boy" his mummy said –
"There's no field, just houses.
it's all in your head."

"But Mummy I see him all of the time
he runs through my dreams
and tells me he's mine."

"My darling Boy, your dreams aren't real
not like the toys you can touch and feel
so go back to bed and I promise you
tomorrow I'll take you to the zoo"

"Ok Mummy, let's do that."
And he goes back to bed while his curtains are shut.

He closes his eyes, mind seeking sleep
and in its dark stillness he hears a voice speak.
Straddling dreams to that place in-between
It whispers the truth of what he has seen.

"I am Horse, that's my field.
I am running free
Forever connected to this place
You see?"

ABOUT THE AUTHOR

Madeleine F White was born in Germany, with roots in Canada and the UK. Having produced a number of national and international web and print magazines, over the last few years she has focussed on being founder/editor of the Write On! suite of publications. As well as being published in a number of magazines and journals, Madeleine has also the authored the 2020 speculative debut novel *Mother Of Floods* and the related audio drama, *The Ark*, reached the top 50 in the Apple podcast charts.

Sea Crow Press

Sea Crow Press is named for a flock of five talkative crows who live on a Cape Cod beach. According to Norse legend, one-eyed Odin sent two crows out into the world so they could return and tell its stories. If you sit and listen to the sea crows as they fly and roost and chatter, it's an easy legend to believe.

An award-winning woman-run independent book publisher based in Massachusetts, Sea Crow Press is committed to amplifying voices that might otherwise go unheard. We publish creative nonfiction, literary fiction, and poetry. Our books celebrate our connection to each other and to the natural world with a focus on positive change and great storytelling.

The *Horse And The Girl* is the first book in a trilogy exploring the spiritual feminine through verse.

ABOUT THE CROSSING PLACES SERIES

The Horse And The Girl is the first book in *The Crossing Places Series*. Life affirming, nurturing and mothering, the series challenges women and our allies to come together to express experiences of the feminine through shared values, ideas and stories in different settings, particularly through nature and the natural world.

Though frame worked by the woman's narrative in *The Horse And The Girl* and the series' second book, *Maiden Mother Crone*, the third and forthcoming book, *The Maiden Mother Crone Anthology*, will give fathers, sons, brothers, partners and colleagues the opportunity to weave their voices and stories in alongside ours.

It is the intention of the Anthology to create space for the expression of feminine values; a shared dialogue that helps catalyse the world we want to build by putting care, empathy, and collaboration at the heart of everything we do.

If you'd like to find out more about The Crossing Places Series or wish to contribute to the anthology, please visit: seacrowpress.com/crossing-places-series

58752434R00047